Original title:
The Friendship Formula

Copyright © 2024 Swan Charm
All rights reserved.

Author: Kätriin Kaldaru
ISBN HARDBACK: 978-9916-89-106-3
ISBN PAPERBACK: 978-9916-89-107-0
ISBN EBOOK: 978-9916-89-108-7

The Essence of Belonging

In quiet corners, hearts unite,
With whispered dreams beneath the night.
A gentle hand, a knowing glance,
In every moment, there's a chance.

We gather 'round the fireside glow,
Tales of our journeys start to flow.
A tapestry of lives we weave,
In shared laughter, we believe.

Through trials faced, our spirits soar,
In every setback, we find more.
Together strong, we stand our ground,
In every heartbeat, love is found.

The bonds we build, so rich and deep,
In every promise that we keep.
A sacred space, where souls connect,
In the essence of respect.

As seasons change, we will remain,
In joy and sorrow, in sun and rain.
For in this circle, we belong,
Together, always, we are strong.

United in Curiosity

Inquiring minds begin to soar,
Through questions asked, we learn much more.
Each answer found, like stars aligned,
Together we seek, as hearts entwined.

A universe unfolds with every peek,
In this vast realm, curiosity speaks.
An endless quest, we boldly chase,
In wonder's light, we find our place.

The Canvas of Kindness

Brush strokes gentle, colors bright,
Kindness paints the world with light.
Each small act, a masterpiece,
In giving hearts, we find our peace.

A warm embrace, a smile shared,
In simple moments, love declared.
With every touch and every word,
The canvas blooms, our spirits stirred.

Sweet Whispers of Understanding

In quiet moments, truth will flow,
Whispers soft, like breezes blow.
Through open hearts, we seek to find,
The threads that bind all humankind.

Empathy blooms in tender grace,
As we explore the human space.
With gentle ears, we hear the plea,
In understanding, we come to be.

The Roots of Connection

Deep in the earth, our roots entwine,
Through shared experiences, so divine.
In every tale, a bond is formed,
In unity's strength, we are transformed.

Like trees that stand against the storm,
Together we thrive, resilient and warm.
Nurtured by love, the branches spread,
In connection's embrace, we are fed.

Compass Points of Connection

In the north, kindness shines bright,
Guiding hearts through the night.
Eastward winds whisper dreams,
Binding souls with gentle beams.

To the south, warmth draws us near,
A sanctuary free of fear.
Westward paths weave tales of old,
In every story, love unfolds.

The Geometry of Together

Lines converge, angles embrace,
In unity, we find our place.
Triangles form in steady hands,
Blueprints drawn on shifting sands.

Circles close, no end in sight,
In shared laughter, we ignite.
Each shape holds a space so true,
A tapestry we weave anew.

A Language of Loyalty

Words unspoken, yet they bind,
In silence, hearts aligned.
Promises crafted in the night,
A gentle bond, forever tight.

In whispers shared with soft intent,
Each moment, a silent testament.
Loyalty, a steadfast flame,
In every breath, we share the same.

Trust: The Constant Variable

In equations of the heart we find,
A constant, gentle and kind.
Variables shift, but trust remains,
Rooted deep, it never wanes.

Through storms of doubt and waves of fear,
Trust anchors us, always near.
In the dance of give and take,
A steadfast bond, the choices we make.

Embracing the Unfamiliar

In shadows cast, we wander wide,
With every step, we leave our guide.
The unknown calls, with whispers sweet,
A dance of dreams, where fears retreat.

In fields of stars, we lose our way,
Yet find the light of a brand new day.
Each stranger's face, a story told,
In laughter shared, our hearts unfold.

Through winding paths, the echoes play,
A symphony of joy, come what may.
We greet the strange with open arms,
Adventure's song, its many charms.

Embracing all, for life's a gift,
In every turn, our spirits lift.
With gratitude, we face the night,
For here we stand, ready for flight.

The Vital Threads

Threads of gold in fabric weave,
Binding hearts, together we cleave.
In silence shared, the world stands still,
With gentle hands, we share our will.

Each laugh a stitch, a careful tie,
In moments brief, we learn to fly.
With tender hearts, we sew our dreams,
Together strong, or so it seems.

Unraveled tales of joy and strife,
We stitch our wounds, we weave our life.
The tapestry of souls entwined,
In every thread, new paths aligned.

From different places, we come anew,
With vibrant hues, a brighter view.
In unity, we find our grace,
The vital threads that time won't erase.

Kindness in the Smallest Acts

A simple smile, a whispered word,
In quiet moments, love is stirred.
A helping hand when darkness falls,
In smallest acts, the heart recalls.

The warmth of tea, the soft embrace,
In moments shared, we find our place.
A note of hope left on a door,
In kindness given, spirits soar.

The little things, often ignored,
Can heal the wounds we can't afford.
A laugh that breaks the heavy night,
In tiny gifts, we share the light.

Through gentle words, we pave the way,
A thread of joy in each new day.
With every step, let kindness reign,
In smallest acts, we break the chain.

Heartbeats in Synchrony

In stillness found, we pulse as one,
With syncopated beats, we run.
A rhythm shared, in every glance,
Two souls entwined in cosmic dance.

The cadence swells, and time stands still,
We chase the dawn with fervent will.
In harmony, our dreams take flight,
With every breath, we draw in light.

The universe hums a soft refrain,
As heartbeats echo, joy and pain.
In every laugh, in every sigh,
Together we stand, never shy.

Through trials faced, our spirits soar,
In perfect sync, we seek for more.
With every pulse, we find our way,
In heartbeats joined, we seize the day.

Unique Coordinates of Companions

In the quiet corners where we meet,
Echoes of laughter, a rhythm sweet.
Footsteps dance on paths we find,
Unique coordinates, hearts aligned.

Threads of connection, woven tight,
Guiding us through the starry night.
In every glance, a spark ignites,
Unique coordinates, pure delights.

Time unfolds like a delicate map,
Each moment shared, a gentle lap.
Together we navigate uncharted seas,
Unique coordinates, just you and me.

Through storms and sun, we roam and play,
Milestones gathered along the way.
Hand in hand, we face the climb,
Unique coordinates, spaces in time.

Our hearts whisper secrets, softly said,
Patterns of friendship, gently spread.
In this vast cosmos, we find our place,
Unique coordinates, a warm embrace.

Moments that Matter

In fleeting instances, life unfolds,
Stories whispered, treasures untold.
A single glance can a lifetime birth,
Moments that matter, treasures of worth.

Silent exchanges, a knowing smile,
The warmth of presence, if just for a while.
In chaos, find a quiet space,
Moments that matter, a tender grace.

Time stretches thin, yet feels so wide,
Each heartbeat echoes, love as our guide.
In laughter shared and tears we share,
Moments that matter, a bond so rare.

Awakened dreams in the morning light,
Footsteps together, hearts taking flight.
With every breath, a purpose clearer,
Moments that matter, love draws us near.

Savor the small, the simple sway,
In daily rhythms, the joy will stay.
Embrace each second that life will scatter,
Moments that matter, always will flatter.

An Equation of Empathy

In the spaces between our words,
Feelings collide, like songbirds.
Understanding whispers in the dark,
An equation of empathy, a heartfelt spark.

Equal measure of joy and pain,
Connection deepened through every strain.
Bridges built with kindness strong,
An equation of empathy, where we belong.

Listening hearts, attentive eyes,
In shared stories, the truth lies.
Every heartbeat marks a score,
An equation of empathy, forever more.

Navigating storms, we learn to bend,
Finding strength in how we mend.
With gentle hands, we will explore,
An equation of empathy, openly soar.

In the calculus of love, we thrive,
Each emotion fuels the drive.
Together we solve, forever entwined,
An equation of empathy, beautifully aligned.

Navigating the Landscape of Love

Across the valleys where feelings grow,
We chart a course in the gentle flow.
Mountains high and rivers wide,
Navigating the landscape of love, side by side.

With every touch, the earth will sigh,
Roots intertwine as seasons fly.
In the soft whispers of the trees,
Navigating the landscape of love, hearts at ease.

Through shifting sands and golden rays,
In tender moments, our spirit plays.
Together we wander, hand in hand,
Navigating the landscape of love, forever planned.

With every star that lights the night,
We find our way with pure delight.
In the quiet speak of the moon above,
Navigating the landscape of love, a gentle shove.

Moments crafted in the softest light,
Together we embrace the beauty in sight.
In gardens rich, our dreams will thrive,
Navigating the landscape of love, alive.

Frequency of Friendship

In laughter shared, our hearts align,
With every smile, the stars will shine.
Through whispers soft and stories told,
A bond like this can't be bought or sold.

In moments shared, we find our way,
Through golden laughs and shades of gray.
Together in silence, a knowing glance,
In the dance of life, we take our chance.

In trials faced, we stand so strong,
With hands held tight, we both belong.
Every heartbeat a song we sing,
In the frequency of friendship, love is king.

Through seasons change, we weather storms,
In every shape, our bond transforms.
With every tear, there's joy to find,
In the melody of hearts entwined.

Forever linked by unspoken ties,
In this realm where true love lies.
With echoes of laughter and moments shared,
In this friendship, we are gladly ensnared.

Touchstones of Trust

In shadows cast, we find our way,
With words like anchors, they guide the play.
A whispered truth, a gentle nod,
In touchstones of trust, we beat the odd.

Through trials faced and mountains high,
We lift each other, we learn to fly.
A pact unbroken, a promise kept,
In the depths of the heart, our secrets slept.

With open arms, we break the fall,
In laughter raised, we stand tall.
United we rise, divided we wait,
In the clasp of trust, we create our fate.

Through time's embrace, we navigate,
In every glance, there's love innate.
With roots so deep, we grow and bloom,
Touchstones of trust, dispelling gloom.

With every heartbeat, a silent vow,
In the tapestry of life, we weave somehow.
Together forged in fires of fate,
Trust is the foundation upon which we create.

Celebrating the Unseen Sparks

In quiet corners, gazes meet,
A spark ignites, a rhythm sweet.
In hushed whispers, secrets fly,
Celebrating the unseen sparks, we sigh.

Each fleeting glance, a gentle grace,
In hidden moments, we find our place.
With every heartbeat, the magic swells,
In the dance of life, the heart compels.

Through tangled paths, we wander near,
In the silent moments, we hold dear.
With dreams entwined, we chase the light,
In the unseen sparks, our souls take flight.

In laughter shared and sighs sincere,
With every moment, love's crystal clear.
Together woven, our spirits spin,
In the beauty of the unseen, we win.

Let's cherish the whispers and tales unvoiced,
In the silent sparks, we rejoice.
In every heartbeat, a love profound,
Celebrating sparks that forever surround.

Wildflowers in a Meadow of Hearts

In a meadow bright, wildflowers bloom,
With colors bold, dispelling gloom.
Each petal soft, a story told,
In the field of hearts, love's grace unfolds.

With every breeze, the blossoms sway,
In daylight's warmth, we laugh and play.
Together we dance, in sunlight's glow,
In the meadow of hearts, our spirits grow.

Through gentle rains, we find our way,
With roots entwined, come what may.
In the beauty of nature, we are one,
Wildflowers thrive under the sun.

Amongst the thorns, we rise above,
In every light, we find our love.
With petals bright, we'll stand apart,
In this meadow of hearts, we'll never part.

With every season, new blooms arise,
In laughter's echo, love never dies.
Through time and space, we'll make our mark,
Wildflowers in a meadow, igniting sparks.

Recipes of Resilience

In the pot of life we blend,
Courage, hope, and time to mend.
Stirred with love, a dash of trust,
Transforming pain into a must.

From ashes rise, our spirits soar,
Each setback brings us back for more.
To taste the strength of every scar,
We find our light, our guiding star.

A sprinkle of joy in each dish,
Vow to nourish every wish.
With every tear, we cook and bake,
Creating dreams, the best we make.

Savoring moments, sweet and tart,
Each bite a whisper from the heart.
Together we gather, side by side,
In this recipe, our hearts abide.

The Spectrum of Shared Joy

In laughter bright, we find our hue,
Moments shared, a vibrant view.
Colors blend, both bold and light,
Igniting souls, our spirits bright.

Each smile paints a scene so grand,
Hands entwined, we understand.
In simple joys, our hearts align,
Creating memories, pure and fine.

Through shades of sorrow, we will tread,
Together, weaving light ahead.
A tapestry of warmth unfurled,
In this spectrum, love is twirled.

In every glance, a spark ignites,
A dance of hope, our shared delights.
Together we build a joyful song,
In unity, we all belong.

Footprints Across Time

Step by step, we wander wide,
Footprints left, where hearts reside.
In sands of time, our story's traced,
Memories linger, never erased.

In the echoes of laughter and tears,
We find the fabric of our years.
Every path, a chapter turns,
In the fire of growth, the spirit burns.

Through seasons changing, we explore,
Each footprint tells of dreams and more.
In every stride, a lesson learned,
A life well-lived, with passions burned.

Together we walk, hand in hand,
Carving tales on this vast land.
With every step, we leave behind,
The stories of souls intertwined.

Guardians of the Heart

In the quiet, we stand as one,
Guardians when the day is done.
With tender care, we lend a hand,
In the shadows, together we stand.

Through trials faced, we hold the light,
Protecting dreams in endless night.
A fortress built with love and trust,
In every heart, we've found our must.

While storms may rage, we won't divide,
In unity, our strength is tied.
Each gentle word, a calming balm,
Together, we create the calm.

As sentinels, our spirits soar,
With every beat, we strive for more.
In this journey, hand in hand,
Guardians true, forever we stand.

Calculating Companionship

In the quiet of the night, we share,
Whispers of dreams in the cool night air.
Numbers dance in the flickering light,
Calculating moments that feel so right.

With every heartbeat, a value to find,
The bonds that tie us, intricately bind.
In laughter and tears, our lives intertwine,
Together we navigate this grand design.

Through trials we face, we stand side by side,
A compass, a guide, as we take the ride.
Equations of trust in the stories we weave,
In the math of friendship, we truly believe.

Every shared glance is a perfect equation,
Fueling the fire of our shared passion.
In the ledger of love, we tally each score,
Each moment cherished, forever explore.

Together we build, with each passing year,
An arithmetic bond that conquers all fear.
In the depths of companionship, we find our way,
A formula of joy that guides us each day.

Harmony in Laughter

In the heart of joy, laughter's song rings,
A melody sweet, and the freedom it brings.
With chuckles and joy, we dance hand in hand,
Creating a symphony, wonderfully grand.

The echoes of laughter fill up the space,
Each giggle a treasure, a warm, sweet embrace.
In the rhythm of life, we find our own beat,
Harmony flowing in moments so sweet.

As sunlight breaks through the clouds in the sky,
Laughter lifts spirits, allowing us to fly.
In joyous connection, we let our hearts soar,
Building a world where sorrow's no more.

With friends all around, we share in delight,
Turning our worries to pure, blissful light.
Each laugh is a note in our life's grand refrain,
Together composing, again and again.

In the dance of our souls, laughter is found,
A binding emotion, beautifully profound.
As long as we share in humor, we'll thrive,
In the garden of laughter, our spirits alive.

Connections in the Cosmos

In the vastness of night, stars shine bright,
Each twinkle a whisper, a beacon of light.
We search for the threads that pull us so near,
Connections unseen, yet incredibly clear.

In cosmic ballet, our paths intertwine,
Galaxies merging, a dance so divine.
Gravity pulls, as we drift through the space,
Together we journey, in infinite grace.

Each moment a spark, igniting the soul,
In the tapestry woven, we quietly scroll.
With echoes of stardust, we trace our own map,
In the universe's arms, we settle and clap.

As we dive through the realms of the unknown,
In the heart of each star, our spirit has grown.
The cosmos whispers secrets, soft as a tune,
In the cradle of night, our hearts speak to the moon.

Together we shine, like constellations aligned,
Bound by a force that is gentle and kind.
In this vast expanse, we find our true place,
Connections in the cosmos, a limitless space.

Synergy of Souls

In the dance of our lives, two souls entwined,
A synergy found that's beautifully defined.
With every heartbeat, we echo as one,
In the warmth of our bond, a new life begun.

Together we rise, like the sun's golden rays,
Illuminating paths through the soft morning haze.
In the depths of our spirits, a fire so bright,
Kindling the warmth that turns darkness to light.

In laughter and silence, we perfectly blend,
Each moment a treasure, with you, my dear friend.
Two voices harmonize, a sweet, soothing sound,
In the embrace of our souls, pure love can be found.

Through trials and triumphs, we weather it all,
In the synergy of souls, we never shall fall.
We'll build our own dreams, layer by layer,
Creating a haven, where hearts can declare.

In unity, we flourish, like flowers in bloom,
Nurtured by love, dispelling all gloom.
As we journey together, the world feels so right,
In the synergy of souls, we find our true light.

Bond Beyond Measure

In the quiet moments we share,
A glance, a smile, a gentle care.
Life's storms may come and sweep along,
But in our hearts, we stay so strong.

Through laughter, tears, we still remain,
United in joy, divided by pain.
With every challenge, hand in hand,
We build our dreams upon this land.

Distance may stretch, but love won't fade,
In every choice, together we wade.
Through the echoes of time, we will stand,
A bond beyond measure, forever grand.

Moments captured, a treasure chest,
In the warmth of trust, we find our rest.
Every heartbeat sings a song,
Together we're right where we belong.

So here's to us, in all we do,
With every dawn, our love feels new.
In this journey, let our hearts seize,
A bond that nurtures, a bond that frees.

Equations of the Heart

In whispers soft, our feelings grow,
Each secret shared, a thread to sew.
Add the laughter, subtract the tears,
In love's algebra, we lose our fears.

X marks the spot where souls entwine,
A formula forged in love divine.
With every moment, we find our way,
Equations of heart lead us astray.

Variables change, yet constants stay,
In your embrace, I long to stay.
Together we solve the puzzles tight,
In the dance of words, our spirits light.

Every touch a number, a cherished sign,
Our hearts beat in harmony, true and fine.
With answers hidden, yet close to see,
You and I, we're our own symphony.

So trust the math that brought us here,
In every heartbeat, I hold you near.
With every glance, our love persists,
Equations of the heart, forever kissed.

Alchemy of Togetherness

In the furnace of life, we ignite,
Transforming dreams into pure light.
We mix our hopes, our fears, our pride,
In the alchemy of love, we abide.

A sprinkle of joy and a dash of grace,
In every moment, we find our place.
With laughter's gold and tears of silver,
Our bond grows deeper, always to deliver.

Through trials faced, we change our fate,
In unity, we find what's great.
With every challenge, our strength we find,
Alchemy of togetherness, ties that bind.

In every heartbeat, a potion brewed,
Together we rise, never subdued.
The magic of us, forever will last,
An elixir potent, our shadows cast.

So let us wander this path of spark,
With open hearts, we leave a mark.
In this dance of life, let our spirits flow,
Alchemy of togetherness, forever aglow.

Threads Woven in Trust

In the tapestry of life we weave,
Threads of our stories, we believe.
Every moment a stitch to bind,
With love at the core, our hearts aligned.

Through colors bright and shadows grey,
In every twist, we find our way.
With hands together, we pull it tight,
Threads woven in trust, pure delight.

Each challenge faced, a lesson learned,
In the furnace of love, we are burned.
Yet still we rise, with patterns new,
Stitching memories, old and true.

In the fabric of time, we stand tall,
Through every season, we won't fall.
With you by my side, I see the light,
Threads woven in trust, shining bright.

So let us celebrate this work of art,
With each new thread, we pour our heart.
In this masterpiece, together we thrive,
Threads woven in trust, keeping love alive.

Embracing Differences

In colors bright, we stand apart,
Each shade a beat, a different heart.
United front, we share our song,
In diversity, we all belong.

Our stories shared, a rich tapestry,
Woven tight in unity.
Through laughter, tears, we learn to see,
The beauty found in you and me.

Each voice a note in life's sweet choir,
We lift each other, rise up higher.
In differences, we find our strength,
Together we can go the length.

A bridge we build from shore to shore,
With open hearts, we crave much more.
Together, side by side we stand,
In harmony, we make our stand.

With open hands, we share the grace,
Embracing all, we find our place.
Together we will face the night,
And in our hearts, let love ignite.

The Joyful Exchange

A smile exchanged beneath the sun,
With simple words, our two hearts run.
In laughter's glow, we chase the day,
Through moments shared, we find our way.

A gift of kindness, small yet bright,
An opened door, a shared delight.
In every glance, a spark of cheer,
Together here, we have no fear.

With hands held tight, we face the song,
In unity, we all belong.
Through ups and downs, our spirits raise,
In joy we dance, through life's sweet maze.

Each story shared, a light we spark,
Illuminating paths, from dawn to dark.
Through the exchange, we find our voice,
In love and laughter, we rejoice.

Together we weave a vibrant thread,
Through every challenge, we forge ahead.
For in this world, we find our range,
In our connection, a joyful exchange.

Hearts in Harmony

Two hearts aligned, in rhythm's sway,
Together we dance, night and day.
In whispers soft, our souls entwined,
In harmony, true friendship finds.

A melody sweet, we sing as one,
Through trials faced, the battles won.
In laughter's echo, our spirits soar,
With open hearts, we seek for more.

When shadows fall, and doubts arise,
We find the light in each other's eyes.
Through every storm, together stand,
In unity, we take command.

A symphony played by hands so kind,
In every moment, true peace we find.
Through thick and thin, we rise above,
In every heartbeat, there's endless love.

To nurture bonds, we learn to share,
In every heartbeat, we show we care.
In perfect tune, we're never apart,
Two souls embracing, one beating heart.

Finding Light in Togetherness

In shadows deep, we seek a spark,
Together we venture, through the dark.
With every step, a guiding flame,
In togetherness, we find our name.

A lantern held, in unity's reach,
With hands entwined, we've much to teach.
Through every challenge, we learn to grow,
In every moment, our hearts aglow.

In stillness shared, and laughter's grace,
We find our strength in this shared space.
Through storms we brave, we hold on tight,
Together we rise, finding our light.

With open arms, we gather near,
In every heartbeat, we conquer fear.
Through every trial, we stand as one,
In togetherness, our day is won.

For in each dawn, a brighter day,
With hope and dreams, we find our way.
In every heartbeat, love guides our flight,
Together we shine, finding our light.

A Circle of Support

In quiet corners, we gather close,
Whispers of strength in a world so vast.
Each hand held tight, a promise we chose,
Together we'll rise, the shadows cast.

With laughter and tears, we paint the sky,
In moments of doubt, we light the way.
Hearts intertwined, we dare to fly,
Together we stand, come what may.

Through storms that threaten, we find our calm,
A refuge where hope can safely bloom.
In the warmth of touch, we find our balm,
Creating a haven, dispelling gloom.

The circle we form is both strong and true,
A tapestry woven from dreams we weave.
In every embrace, our spirits renew,
A bond unbroken, a way to believe.

So here's to the love that we freely share,
In the circle of support, we're never alone.
Embracing our journeys, we show we care,
With hearts wide open, we find our home.

Starlit Conversations

Beneath the sky where the cosmos gleams,
We speak in whispers, soft as night.
Stars align with our secret dreams,
Illuminating paths of shared delight.

The moon listens close to tales we weave,
Each moment, a treasure spun from the dark.
In silence, we find the strength to believe,
A universe scattered with love's bright spark.

With every breath, we unlock the vast,
Words like constellations, guiding our way.
In the tapestry of now and past,
We find our solace, come what may.

As shadows dance in a gentle breeze,
We plant the seeds of who we'll become.
In starlit moments, the heart finds ease,
Through every story, our souls feel numb.

So let us linger, just you and I,
In these midnight talks that softly flow.
With every glance, we reach for the sky,
In the warmth of connection, we always grow.

Unraveling the Ties That Bind

In tangled threads, our stories lie,
Knots of heartache, joy, and fears.
We seek the light, let courage fly,
Unraveling truths across the years.

Each layer pulled reveals a tale,
Of struggles faced and lessons learned.
With every tug, we find the hail,
Of brighter days, our spirits yearned.

In moments paused, we breathe it in,
The messiness of love so real.
With patience, slowly, we begin,
To weave anew, our fate to seal.

For every bond, a choice we make,
Through trials faced, we find our way.
Though ties may fray, we won't forsake,
The strength inside that guides our sway.

Together we rise, through thick and thin,
Our hearts linked tight, we choose to mend.
With every thread, we let love win,
Unraveling pain, as we transcend.

Echoes of Heartbeats

In the quiet spaces, whispers dwell,
The echo of heartbeats, soft and near.
Rhythms of life that stories tell,
In the stillness, love shines clear.

With every thump, we find our grace,
A symphony played in the night's embrace.
In the dance of shadows, we trace,
Every moment held, a sacred space.

Through laughter and sighs, we intertwine,
The pulse of connection, a tapestry spun.
In the depth of silence, our hearts align,
Beating together, two souls as one.

In echoes that linger, memories thrive,
Each heartbeat a promise, a bond so true.
Through trials faced, we strive to survive,
In the rhythm of life, it's me and you.

So let us listen, to the sounds we make,
In the chorus of love, we'll always be found.
With echoes of heartbeats, foundations we break,
In harmony's embrace, forever spellbound.

The Heat of Shared Fires

In the glow of embers bright,
Stories drift into the night.
Voices blend, wise and warm,
Hearts unite in tales reborn.

Laughter dances through the air,
A tapestry of memories rare.
Together, shadows intertwine,
In this moment, all is fine.

Flickering flames, a gentle guide,
In the hush, our dreams confide.
With each crackle, hope ignites,
Bonding souls in soft delights.

We share the warmth, the light we crave,
A circle tight, our spirits brave.
The night is ours, the stars align,
In the heat of fires, hearts entwine.

Synchronized Heartbeats

Two hearts beat in perfect time,
A rhythm deep, a soulful chime.
In the quiet, pulses race,
Connected in this sacred space.

Every breath a whispered song,
In harmony, we belong.
Hands entwined, we weave the night,
In synchronized love's gentle light.

Moments pass, yet time stands still,
A bond so strong, it bends the will.
With every thump, a promise made,
In this dance, we are unafraid.

In gentle silence, love concedes,
The heart speaks more than words or deeds.
With every glance, we understand,
Together, forever, hand in hand.

Connections in the Quiet

In stillness, whispers softly share,
A bond unseen, a treasure rare.
Listening close, we feel the stir,
In quiet moments, hearts confer.

Between the breaths, a world is spun,
Threads of fate, weaving as one.
Silence holds the truth we seek,
In subtle glances, love can speak.

The night enfolds us, dreams take flight,
In every pause, love ignites.
Through gentle shadows, we connect,
In the stillness, we reflect.

No need for words, the world outside,
Together here, we can confide.
In the quiet, bonds take shape,
In this silence, hearts escape.

Bonds Beyond Borders

Across the miles, our spirits soar,
A connection deep, forever more.
Though lands divide, hearts stay close,
In love's embrace, we find our hope.

Messages carried on the breeze,
In every moment, hearts find ease.
Time and space cannot confine,
These bonds we share, intertwined.

With every smile that breaks the day,
Distance fades in love's ballet.
Like rivers merge, our paths align,
In every heartbeat, souls entwine.

Through laughter shared, we bridge the gap,
In every hug, we close the map.
Together strong, we rise and strive,
Bonds unbroken, love alive.

Navigating Through Storms

Waves crash high, winds scream loud,
Fear grips tight, amidst the crowd.
Yet in the dark, a light may gleam,
Hope's faint whisper, a daring dream.

With sturdy helm, I steer my course,
Facing the tempest, gathering force.
Each drop of rain, a story shared,
Through storms we rise, together prepared.

The clouds may darken, shadows may fall,
But in this journey, we stand tall.
Friendship's anchor, strong and true,
Guides us safely, me and you.

Navigating tides, both rough and calm,
Finding strength in each other's balm.
When thunder rumbles, we won't despair,
For in unity, there's always care.

Through every squall, our hearts entwine,
With every break, our spirits shine.
Together we sail, through night and day,
Navigating storms, come what may.

Sails of Support

In quiet waters, sails unfurl,
With gentle breezes, dreams do swirl.
Tethered to hope, we start to glide,
With sails of support, we will not hide.

Through straits unknown, with you I roam,
Find strength in laughter, make it home.
When storms arise, and tempests roar,
Our bond, a beacon, forevermore.

The winds may shift, but hearts stay true,
In every challenge, standing with you.
With every gust, new tales to tell,
In sails of support, we flourish well.

Navigating life, we find our way,
With love as compass, we'll never sway.
Braving the waves, joys we'll explore,
Each moment cherished, forevermore.

Together we sail, through thick and thin,
With sails of support, we always win.
In calm and tempest, steadfast we stand,
Navigating seas, hand in hand.

Illuminated Journeys

In twilight's glow, we make our start,
Footsteps echo, a beating heart.
Glow of lanterns, guiding the way,
Illuminated dreams, come what may.

With every mile, new sights will show,
Whispers of wisdom, soft and slow.
Paths intertwine, with tales to share,
Lighting the journey, love in the air.

Through winding roads and timeless trees,
We find our strength, simple as these.
Guided by stars, and moon's embrace,
Illuminated journeys, a sacred space.

Each moment treasured, every laugh a song,
In this adventure, we all belong.
With every heartbeat, our spirits soar,
Illuminated by love, forevermore.

With lights aglow, we journey bright,
Hand in hand, through day and night.
Together we wander, a vision so clear,
Illuminated journeys, always near.

Buds of Camaraderie

In springtime's breath, new friendships grow,
As buds of camaraderie start to show.
With warmth and laughter, colors unite,
In this garden of joy, hearts take flight.

Through vibrant fields, together we roam,
Each blooming smile, a token of home.
With every petal, memories sown,
In the bonds we nurture, love has grown.

Through sun and rain, we weather it all,
With hands interwoven, we stand tall.
The fragrance of trust, sweet and pure,
In buds of camaraderie, we endure.

With whispers of hope and dreams we share,
We cultivate joy, and banish despair.
As seasons change, our roots intertwine,
Buds of camaraderie, forever divine.

In life's great garden, we'll thrive and bloom,
In friends we find light, dispelling the gloom.
Through every moment, together we strive,
In buds of camaraderie, we come alive.

A Tapestry of Trust

In threads of gold we weave our ties,
With every word, a voice that flies.
A bond so strong, it will not break,
In shadows cast, the light we make.

Through whispered dreams, we share our fears,
In laughter bright, we dry our tears.
A tapestry of hearts entwined,
In every stitch, our souls aligned.

Through trials faced, we stand as one,
In moments shared, we've just begun.
With faith as strong as woven lace,
In trust, we find our sacred space.

With open hearts, we take the leap,
In kindness sown, the roots run deep.
Together we create a home,
Where love and trust have freely grown.

So here we stand, come rain or shine,
In every heartbeat, you are mine.
A tapestry, forever bright,
In love's embrace, we find our light.

Shared Secrets Under the Moon

In twilight's hush, the world stands still,
With whispered dreams that give us thrill.
Beneath the stars, our secrets flow,
In shadows cast, our truths we show.

The moonlit path, a guiding light,
As we confide in the deep of night.
With every glance, a story told,
In every heartbeat, courage bold.

Through tangled thoughts, we find our way,
In soft-spoken words, we gently sway.
The bond we share, a sacred thread,
With every secret, mountains tread.

In laughter shared, the night takes flight,
We dance with dreams and hold on tight.
Together we weave an endless tale,
In moonlit whispers, we shall not fail.

So here we stand, no fear of dark,
In friendship forged, we leave our mark.
With every secret, trust will bloom,
A garden grown beneath the moon.

The Dance of Kindness

With gentle steps, we move as one,
In every act, our hearts have spun.
A dance of grace, where spirits soar,
In kindness shared, we offer more.

With open hands, we lift the weak,
In every smile, the warmth we seek.
Through simple deeds, we change the course,
A ripple formed, a mighty force.

In every moment, love's embrace,
With tender hearts, we find our place.
Through trials faced, we hold each other,
In kindness shown, we are life's mother.

The rhythm flows, a soothing balm,
In times of storm, our hearts stay calm.
With every step, we light the way,
A dance of kindness, come what may.

So let us twirl beneath the skies,
With every gesture, love will rise.
In perfect harmony, we find our song,
In this sweet dance, we all belong.

Bridges Built on Joy

Across the chasm, wide and deep,
We build the bridges, dreams to keep.
With laughter bright as morning light,
In joy we find our shared delight.

With every stone that's placed with care,
A pathway forged, we freely share.
In moments small, our hearts unite,
With every step, we reach new heights.

In melody, our voices blend,
Through every note, our spirits mend.
With open arms, we welcome new,
In joy's embrace, we start anew.

As seasons turn, our laughter grows,
In pain and joy, our true love shows.
The bridges built, a testament,
In every moment, time is spent.

So let us dance on paths we've made,
In every heart, our dreams cascade.
With bridges built, we stand as one,
In joy we find life's endless run.

The Warmth of Togetherness

In quiet corners, shadows dance,
Hearts entwined, we take our chance.
A smile exchanged, a knowing glance,
Together, we find our circumstance.

The laughter echoes, sweet and clear,
In every moment, you are near.
Through storms and sun, we show no fear,
The warmth of love, our greatest tier.

Hand in hand, we face the world,
With every challenge, flags unfurled.
In your embrace, my dreams are swirled,
Together strong, our lives are twirled.

Memories woven, deep and vast,
In every heartbeat, echoes cast.
We build a future, strong and fast,
With love to guide, we're unsurpassed.

As seasons change, we stand as one,
Chasing horizons, where dreams run.
In the tapestry, threads are spun,
Forever bright, our journey's begun.

Paths Intertwined

Two roads converge beneath the trees,
And whispers rustle with the breeze.
In every step, we share the ease,
Of finding joy in memories.

Side by side, our stories blend,
With every twist, we comprehend.
In silent moments, hearts extend,
A bond unbroken, we transcend.

Through winding trails and paths unknown,
We carve a space, we call our own.
In laughter shared, our love has grown,
Together facing the overgrown.

The footprints linger on the ground,
In our embrace, the world is found.
With every heartbeat, love profound,
In unity, our souls are bound.

Seasons shift, but we remain,
In every sunshine, in every rain.
With hands clasped tight, we'll bear the strain,
Our paths entwined, love's sweet refrain.

A Compass of Compassion

In moments dark, your light will shine,
A guiding star, a love divine.
With open hearts, our paths align,
Through every struggle, we define.

Compassion blooms in gentle ways,
In quiet acts, our hearts ablaze.
With every kindness, life displays,
A compass pointing, through the haze.

When shadows fall, and spirits wane,
We lift each other, share the pain.
In unity, our strength we gain,
Through storms and sun, the love remains.

With every word, we sow the seeds,
Of understanding, meeting needs.
A tapestry, of shared good deeds,
Compassion's thread is what it breeds.

Together, we will forge the way,
With hope and warmth, we'll seize the day.
In every heart, a bright bouquet,
A compass of compassion, here to stay.

The Magic of Shared Moments

In fleeting glimpses, time stands still,
A secret thrill, a joyous thrill.
In laughter shared, we find our will,
The magic grows, with every chill.

Our hands entwined, we chase the sun,
In every moment, we have won.
With every heartbeat, joy's begun,
A tapestry of love, we've spun.

Through whispered dreams and midnight talks,
In gentle strolls, on silent walks.
The magic in the way love stalks,
Through hidden paths and quiet flocks.

When stars ignite the velvet night,
In soft embraces, pure delight.
With every glance, the world feels right,
In shared moments, our hearts take flight.

Together, we create a song,
A melody that carries strong.
In every heartbeat, we belong,
The magic of our love—prolonged.

Bonds that Defy Distance

Across the miles, our hearts entwine,
A thread unseen, yet strong and fine.
In whispered words, we bridge the gap,
In silent dreams, we share the map.

Through time zones vast, our laughter flows,
In every text, the affection grows.
No length can sever what we embrace,
Our spirits dance in a cherished space.

A voice can reach, despite the night,
And in the dark, you are my light.
We count the days till we are near,
In every heartbeat, love will steer.

Though oceans wide may lie between,
Our souls connect, a vivid scene.
In every moment, we hold tight,
Through passing days and sleepless nights.

So here's to bonds that never fade,
In every call, my heart's conveyed.
We are the stars that brightly shine,
A galaxy of love, divine.

Unwritten Codes of Care

In every glance, a secret shared,
An unspoken pact, a love declared.
Through gentle gestures, our stories weave,
A tapestry of trust, hard to conceive.

We dance in silence, a subtle rhythm,
Finding comfort in our quiet system.
With every nod, a promise made,
In this silent bond, no feelings fade.

Through trials faced, we stand as one,
In every battle, we've already won.
A language formed, without a sound,
In caring hearts, our strength is found.

With every tear that's softly shed,
In shared sorrows, our hearts are fed.
No need for words to show we care,
In silent strength, our love lays bare.

So here's to codes that never break,
In every choice, our hearts awake.
Together always, we shall thrive,
In unwritten love, we come alive.

Synapses of Support

Like pathways formed in our minds,
We build connections of the best kinds.
In every thought, a lift, a push,
Through warm embraces, we feel the rush.

With every struggle, you show the way,
In darkest nights, you light the day.
Your words are sparks that help ignite,
The strength within, to brace the fight.

We weave a net of hope and grace,
In every challenge, we find our place.
Your hand in mine, we face the storm,
In unity, our hearts transform.

Through every setback, we will grow,
In kindness shared, our spirits glow.
In bonds of steel, our dreams take flight,
With every heartbeat, we unite.

So here's to networks made with care,
In every struggle, we are aware.
Together we rise, we'll never stand,
As pillars of growth, we take command.

The Symmetry of Shared Moments

In fleeting seconds, we find our grace,
In every laugh, a familiar face.
Through moments shared, our souls align,
Each memory crafted is truly divine.

From quiet talks to joyful screams,
In every heartbeat, we share dreams.
Each glance exchanged tells stories untold,
In vibrant hues, our lives unfold.

In sunsets watched, side by side,
In gentle whispers, our hopes confide.
Through every tear and every cheer,
The fabric of love is stitched so clear.

With every parting, new paths we chase,
Yet in our hearts, there's always space.
For all the laughter, all the pain,
In unity, we grow once again.

So here's to moments we call our own,
In every trial, our seeds are sown.
Together we stand, forever tied,
In the symmetry where love resides.

Kindred Spirits in Bloom

In gardens where the wildflowers grow,
Two souls entwined, a gentle glow.
With whispers soft, they share their dreams,
A world of magic, or so it seems.

Through sunlit days and starry nights,
Their laughter dances, pure delight.
In every petal, love takes flight,
As kindred spirits bloom so bright.

The seasons change, yet they remain,
In vibrant hues, through joy and pain.
A bond unbroken, ever strong,
In nature's chorus, they belong.

With every breeze, their secrets share,
A whispered promise hangs in air.
In moments still, their hearts align,
In timeless beauty, they combine.

Together as they dance and sway,
An endless journey, come what may.
For hand in hand, they always bloom,
In gardens vast, they find their room.

Echoes of Laughter

In twilight's glow, old stories rise,
With echoes of laughter, filling skies.
Each memory shines like stars at night,
A joyous tapestry, woven tight.

Around the fire, friends gather near,
Sharing the tales they hold so dear.
With every chuckle, a spark ignites,
In warmth and love, the heart unites.

Through ups and downs, they weather storms,
In every heartbeat, friendship warms.
The lightness lingers, a soft embrace,
Together always, in joyous space.

In gentle moments, laughter swells,
Creating bonds that time compels.
In shared delight, the world's aglow,
Echoes of laughter, forever flow.

In days gone by and those to come,
Their laughter sings, a mellifluous hum.
In memory's hall, they shall reside,
With echoes of laughter as their guide.

Threads That Bind

In quiet corners, whispers meet,
With threads that bind, a tapestry sweet.
Each story shared, a woven strand,
Together they grow, hand in hand.

Through trials faced, and joys embraced,
In every heart, their love is traced.
With colors bright, yet shadows cast,
They stitch the future from the past.

In moments tender, their spirits soar,
With laughter echoing, they explore.
While time may fray the edges bold,
Their bond holds strong, a tale retold.

In gentle threads, their lives entwine,
A work of art, forever fine.
Through years ahead, they'll often find,
Together always, threads that bind.

With heartstrings pulled, they find the song,
In unity, they both belong.
In harmony, they weave the light,
Threads that bind, a pure delight.

Navigating Life's Tides

Beneath the moon, the waters sway,
Navigating life, come what may.
With every wave, new paths unfold,
A journey painted, brave and bold.

In tempest storms, they find their way,
With steadfast hearts, they choose to stay.
Through shifting sands and rocky shores,
Together always, love endures.

With compass true, they chart their course,
In harmony, they find their force.
Through every ebb and every flow,
In gentle currents, their spirit grows.

In sun-kissed moments, joy ignites,
With laughter bright, their hope excites.
Through life's vast ocean, hand in hand,
They navigate the shifting sand.

And when the night brings quiet peace,
Their hearts will whisper, fears release.
For through each tide, they shall abide,
Together strong, life's joyful ride.

Gazes That Speak

In a room where silence swells,
Two eyes collide, a story tells.
Words unspoken, emotions bright,
In that gaze, we find our light.

The world fades, it's just us two,
Every glance, a memory new.
Expressions dance, hearts learn to play,
In radiant hues, love finds its way.

Shadows whisper, and time suspends,
In stolen glances, connection mends.
With every blink, a promise made,
In gentle stares, our fears allayed.

Moments shared, the air ignites,
Lost in thoughts and lingering sights.
A language pure, without a sound,
In gazes deep, our truths are found.

In this realm where silence reigns,
Two souls echo in sweet refrains.
With every look, our hearts will leap,
In the language of gazes, we speak.

Harmonies of the Heart

In the quiet of the night,
Softly hums a tune of light.
Melodies weave in gentle flows,
A symphony that only grows.

Notes of warmth, a lover's sigh,
In the stillness, hearts reply.
Together swaying, side by side,
In harmony, we choose to bide.

Every heartbeat, a rhythm dear,
In this dance, we cast out fear.
A chorus found in tender grace,
With each touch, we find our place.

Soft whispers ride the evening breeze,
In every note, our souls feel ease.
When life plays on, and storms may part,
We'll find refuge in our heart.

In the echoes, love will stand,
Creating bonds that time can't strand.
Together, as the music sings,
Our hearts will soar on unseen wings.

Treasured Laughs

In the sunlight's warming rays,
Laughter dances, vibrant plays.
Every chuckle, a treasure true,
In shared moments, joy breaks through.

Stories weave in playful jest,
A melody that feels the best.
With every giggle, spirits rise,
In these moments, love never lies.

The world feels lighter, hearts set free,
In laughter's embrace, just you and me.
A bond forged in mirth's sweet glow,
In every smile, our happiness grows.

From whispered jokes to boisterous cheer,
We craft memories, year by year.
In every laugh, a spark ignites,
As we dance through life's delights.

So let us laugh until we cry,
With each shared joke, let time fly by.
For in these laughs, our souls entwine,
In this joyful dance, forever shine.

Bonds Like Fables

In tales of old, where magic sways,
Our bond is written in golden ways.
Stories woven through time and space,
In every chapter, you find your place.

Like whispered dreams under starlit skies,
In every page, our love defies.
With each adventure, hand in hand,
We craft a story, bold and grand.

In the echoes of laughter clear,
Our hearts compose a truth sincere.
Through trials faced and joys experienced,
Together we flourish, our spirits dance.

The winds may howl, and shadows cast,
Yet in this fable, our love will last.
Forever bright, a timeless song,
In the book of life, where we belong.

So turn the page, and let us write,
A narrative full of pure delight.
In every twist, fate intertwines,
With bonds like fables, our love shines.

The Alchemy of Laughter

Laughter dances on the breeze,
A spark igniting joy with ease.
In shared moments, hearts collide,
Transforming pain, casting it aside.

With every giggle, we create,
A potion sweet to elevate.
In mirthful echoes, we'll remain,
A bond unbroken through joy and pain.

Cascading laughter, pure delight,
Illuminating darkest night.
In this alchemy, we find grace,
Together, time we can embrace.

We pour our hearts into each joke,
As laughter's balm begins to cloak.
It soothes the soul, heals the scar,
A treasured gift, our guiding star.

Through giggles shared, our spirits rise,
Two kindred souls beneath the skies.
In every chuckle, magic stirs,
As laughter's song, the world prefers.

Weaving Hearts Together

Threads of kindness, woven tight,
In every heart, a gentle light.
With every stitch, our stories blend,
Creating paths that never end.

In moments shared, we craft a tapestry,
Of laughter, tears, and sweet memory.
Through joys and sorrows, hand in hand,
We find our footing, understand.

With colors bright, our lives entwine,
In every pattern, love will shine.
Weaving hearts, a sacred art,
Together we mend, never apart.

Frayed edges meet, we pull and tug,
Sewing warmth with every hug.
In this fabric, we find our song,
A harmony where we belong.

Each gentle knot binds us anew,
In this journey, me and you.
With threads of trust, we'll carry through,
A masterpiece that's always true.

Companions in the Stars

Underneath the cosmic tide,
Together, we will seek and stride.
In constellation's gentle glow,
Side by side, our spirits flow.

With stardust dreams, we chase the night,
Guided by the silver light.
Each pulse of warmth ignites the sky,
As whispers of the universe sigh.

Through timeless realms, we laugh and share,
The secrets hidden, laid bare.
With every glance, we map the heights,
In unity, we chase new sights.

Galaxies spin as we explore,
In our hearts, we long for more.
Companions bound by fate's own stream,
Together chasing every dream.

In the vastness, our spirits soar,
Navigating the cosmic floor.
Forever caught in heaven's dance,
In starlit paths, we take our chance.

The Art of Understanding

To listen deep, to feel and see,
The soul's whisper, fragile plea.
In silence shared, we find the key,
Unlocking hearts, you and me.

With open minds, we bridge the gap,
In gentle words, we lay the map.
Compassion blooms where kindness grows,
In understanding, love bestows.

Each story told, a tapestry,
Of how we're woven, you and me.
Through empathy, we learn to feel,
A truth unmasked, a shared appeal.

In this dance of give and take,
We nurture bonds that never break.
Through patience, we seek to comprehend,
In every heart, we find a friend.

So let us cherish this sweet art,
For understanding paves the heart.
In every moment, let us strive,
To hold each other, to truly thrive.

Lanterns in the Dark

In the night, a glow appears,
Guiding lost souls, calming fears.
Lanterns flicker, softly bright,
Their warm light chases away the night.

Beneath the stars, they weave a dance,
Whispers of hope, a fleeting chance.
Each flicker tells a tale untold,
Of dreams and wishes, brave and bold.

In the shadows, magic brews,
Lighting paths with vivid hues.
Every lantern, a guiding spark,
Illuminates the softest dark.

Together they form a starry sea,
Bonding hearts, setting spirits free.
Through the haze, they mark the way,
Until the dawn of a brand new day.

So let them shine, these lights so dear,
In every heart, may love appear.
For in the dark, we find our part,
With lanterns bright, we brave the heart.

Heart Strings Attached

A melody flows, soft and sweet,
Pulling at heartstrings, in rhythmic beat.
Whispers of love, in every thread,
Binding souls, where words are said.

In the silence, we hear the sound,
Of laughter echoed, love unbound.
With each note, we weave our fate,
In this dance, we celebrate.

Tangled in moments, rich and rare,
Every glance speaks, a tender care.
From heart to heart, the music plays,
Guiding us through the winding maze.

Strumming chords of memories made,
In the tapestry, love won't fade.
Holding on, we hum along,
In this bond, we both belong.

So let the song linger in the air,
With every beat, show that we care.
Together in rhythm, never apart,
We weave our lives, heartstrings and art.

The Mosaic of Friendship

A tapestry woven, bright and bold,
Each piece a story, waiting to be told.
Colors of laughter, shades of tears,
In this mosaic, we conquer our fears.

With every shard, a memory clear,
Binding us closer, through every year.
In the light, our friendship shines,
A canvas of love, through sacred signs.

Fragments of moments, scattered around,
Making a picture, where joy is found.
Each bit a treasure, each hue a smile,
Crafting a journey, mile after mile.

Through storms we weather, side by side,
In the heart's gallery, we take our stride.
Cherished connections, we will defend,
A beautiful puzzle, our hearts to mend.

So let's create, as time goes by,
With each new piece, let spirits fly.
In the mosaic of friendship's art,
We find our place, we play our part.

Gentle Waves of Affection

In the stillness, waters sigh,
Caressing shores as moments fly.
Gentle waves, a kiss so soft,
Embracing hearts, lifting them aloft.

Each ripple carries whispers sweet,
Brushing against our longing feet.
In the ebb and flow, love begins,
Washing away all worries and sins.

Under the sun, they dance and gleam,
Reflecting hopes, like a distant dream.
With every crash, a promise made,
In this embrace, our fears will fade.

Together we float on this sea so wide,
In currents strong, we find our guide.
With gentle tides, our hearts will sway,
In the moonlight, we find our way.

So let the waves roll in with grace,
Filling our lives, a warm embrace.
With every splash, new love will flow,
In gentle waves, our feelings grow.

Conversations Across the Ocean

Waves carry whispers from far away,
Voices ride currents, night turns to day.
Messages float on an endless breeze,
Hearts intertwined across calm seas.

Moonlight dances on the water's crest,
Dreams painted bright, souls find their rest.
Each word a bridge, each laugh a wave,
Bringing together the hearts we crave.

Silhouettes cast on the horizon wide,
In the silence, our spirits abide.
Across the distance, we'll find a way,
To share our truths in the light of day.

As tides swell, so do our hopes,
Navigating life, we learn to cope.
In every wave, a story unfolds,
Friendship precious, more than gold.

Together we stand, though miles apart,
An ocean of trust connects every heart.
Beneath the stars, our souls fly free,
In these conversations, we seem to be.

The Strength of Many

A circle of hands, both strong and kind,
Together we rise, new dreams in mind.
Voices united, a powerful song,
In the strength of many, we all belong.

Mountains may tremble, but we stand tall,
Together we answer when duty calls.
Each heartbeat echoes the rhythm of hope,
With unity's force, we learn to cope.

Through storms we weather, we grow and learn,
In the fires of struggle, we brightly burn.
Each individual shines with a light,
Illuminating paths in the darkest night.

From whispers of courage, our spirits will soar,
For in collaboration, there's always more.
Together we build, together we climb,
In the strength of many, we conquer time.

With open arms, we welcome the new,
Sharing our wisdom, so much to pursue.
Beyond the horizon, our vision expands,
In the strength of many, we join our hands.

Through Thick and Thin

Life's winding road, with all its bends,
It's the journey that shapes us, the love that mends.
Through laughter and tears, we stand side by side,
In the warmth of our bond, we find our pride.

When shadows fall and dreams may fade,
We lift each other, never afraid.
In moments of silence, our hearts still speak,
For in gentle whispers, we're never weak.

Through storms we weather, both fierce and bold,
In stories of comfort, our truths are told.
With hope as our anchor, we shall not sway,
Together we conquer the darkest of days.

In each little triumph, we find our light,
Supporting each other, our spirits ignite.
In the dance of life, we give and receive,
Through thick and thin, together we believe.

When the world gets rough and burdens grow heavy,
We walk through the fire, our hearts ever ready.
With hands intertwined, we'll always endure,
For the love that we share is forever pure.

Soulful Resonance

In the quiet moments, our spirits dance,
Music of the heart, in every glance.
Melodies woven through the fabric of time,
In the depths of silence, our souls align.

Each note a whisper, each chord a sigh,
Echoes of love that never say goodbye.
Through trials we journey, we find our song,
In this soulful resonance, we all belong.

With every heartbeat, a rhythm of grace,
In the tapestry of life, we find our place.
Together we harmonize, voices entwined,
Creating a symphony of the divine.

In laughter and tears, we share the weight,
A chorus of feelings, we celebrate fate.
United in spirit, we rise and soar,
With soulful resonance, we'll seek for more.

When shadows gather and the light feels dim,
We'll rise like the dawn, with hope that won't swim.
In every connection, music will bloom,
For in soul's resonance, we dispel the gloom.

The Missing Piece of Kindness

In a world that sometimes feels gray,
A gentle touch can light the way.
Small gestures bloom like springtime flowers,
Brightening hearts in quiet hours.

With every smile, a bond we weave,
A simple act, and we believe.
Kindness travels through the air,
Creating warmth, a love to share.

In moments lost, we find our place,
An open heart, a soft embrace.
When shadows linger, hope is near,
The missing piece, we hold it dear.

To give, to share, to understand,
A tiny spark can start a band.
Together strong, we'll make it clear,
That kindness is what we hold most dear.

So take a moment, pause and see,
The power wrapped in empathy.
For in this life, when we align,
The missing piece is love, divine.

Patterns of Understanding

In the tapestry of hearts we bind,
Patterns emerge, in threads we find.
Each story told, a shade of truth,
Woven with care, a shared youth.

Listening close, we break the wall,
In hues of wisdom, we stand tall.
Every point of view, a unique thread,
Connecting all, where journeys led.

With open minds, our worlds expand,
Finding rhythm in a delicate strand.
The more we learn, the more we grow,
Understanding flares, a gentle glow.

For every soul holds a secret key,
Unlocking doors to harmony.
With patience, we will find the way,
Patterns of love in bright display.

So let us dance in this embrace,
Intertwined in a sacred space.
Together we'll paint a vibrant land,
In patterns, hearts will learn to stand.

Seeds of Shared Smiles

In gardens rich with gentle grace,
Seeds of joy begin to trace.
Each smile shared, a flower grows,
In every heart, a warmth bestows.

With laughter light, we break the night,
Together bloom, a pure delight.
Cultivating joy, hand in hand,
In this world, we understand.

Through trials faced, our roots run deep,
In kindness sown, our dreams we keep.
Each shared glance, a bond anew,
In shared smiles, we find the true.

As seasons change, our blooms will sway,
In harmony, we'll find our way.
Through sunshine, rain, our spirits climb,
A garden grown, transcending time.

So plant the seeds where love can thrive,
And watch the beauty come alive.
In every smile, a story beams,
Together we're the wildest dreams.

The Architecture of Affection

In every brick of trust we lay,
A fortress blooms, keeping fears at bay.
With every smile, our foundation grows,
In the heart's design, pure love flows.

Together we sketch a life so grand,
Every line drawn with a steady hand.
In the rafters, laughter rings true,
The architecture holds me and you.

With patience measured, we craft each room,
Filled with warmth, dispelling gloom.
Each corner whispers secrets shared,
In spaces built, we showed we cared.

As beams of hope stretch towards the light,
We find our way through darkest night.
In this shelter, we stand tall,
Constructed strong, we'll never fall.

So let's design our dreams anew,
With every heart, we'll see it through.
A masterpiece of love, no less,
In the architecture of tenderness.

Beyond the Surface: A Deeper Dive

To venture deep beneath the waves,
Where light and shadows gently play.
The ocean's whisper softly saves,
The secrets hidden in the sway.

In currents strong, we find our strength,
A world alive, the heartbeats thrum.
With every stroke, we go the length,
Connected in the vastness, come.

In depths where silence speaks so loud,
The colors bloom, the fish will glide.
Amongst the coral, not too proud,
We find the beauty, deep inside.

Each creature has a tale to tell,
In harmony, we intertwine.
In this abyss, we bid farewell,
To surface dreams and seek the divine.

So dive with me, in waters clear,
For love's an ocean, wide and deep.
Together, casting off all fear,
In this embrace, forever keep.

Infinite Threads

In every stitch, a story lives,
A tapestry of joy and pain.
We weave with care, as time forgives,
Each thread a love that shall remain.

The colors blend, both bright and dark,
A portrait rich, the heart displays.
Each moment crafts a vibrant mark,
As life unfolds in myriad ways.

Through twists and turns, the patterns form,
Our hands, they guide the fabric's flow.
In every storm, we find the warm,
In threads of gold, our spirits grow.

With trust, we stitch the seams of fate,
A bond unbreakable, we find.
In laughter shared or quiet state,
The weave of us, two hearts aligned.

Forever formed in hues divine,
Together, we embrace the change.
In every thread, our lives entwine,
A masterpiece in love's exchange.

Finite Moments

A fleeting glance, a breath in time,
The clock ticks softly, hearts collide.
In memories made, we find the rhyme,
Within these moments, love can't hide.

Each second counts, a precious gift,
In laughter shared or silent sighs.
Through tender hearts, our spirits lift,
Life's simple joy, beneath the skies.

As seasons change, we cling to now,
The past a whisper, dreams unfold.
In finite time, we make our vow,
To write a tale that won't grow old.

In every glance, a thousand dreams,
In every touch, a spark ignites.
We dance like leaves in sunlight beams,
These moments cherished, pure delights.

So let us savor every breath,
In every heartbeat, let love dwell.
For life is brief, yet love is depth,
In finite moments, we are blessed.

The Tapestry of Us

In threads of laughter, we are bound,
A tapestry of hopes and fears.
In moments shared, our joys resound,
As time weaves on through all the years.

Each pattern tells a tale so bright,
Of journeys walked and lessons learned.
In every shade, we find the light,
From woven love, our passion burned.

With colors bold, we paint our dreams,
In vibrant hues that dance and play.
Through ups and downs, our spirit screams,
In every thread, we find our way.

Together, crafting with our hands,
An artwork forged through deep resolve.
Through life's embrace, as each heart stands,
In the tapestry, we evolve.

So let us weave, entwined as one,
With every stitch, our souls unite.
In this creation, never done,
The tapestry of us shines bright.

Variables of Affection

In every heart, a shuffle plays,
A dance of feelings, in the night.
Emotions shift in wondrous ways,
As love takes flight, a pure delight.

With every glance, the sparks ignite,
In whispers soft, the secrets flow.
The variables, a heart's true sight,
In moments shared, affection grows.

Through sunlight bright and shadowed lanes,
We navigate this maze of trust.
In laughter's echo, joy remains,
Through gentle words, in love we must.

For in connections, layers hide,
A spectrum rich, in shades we find.
Through storms and calm, we turn the tide,
In variables, our hearts aligned.

So let us dance in love's embrace,
In every heartbeat, find our song.
For in this journey, face to face,
The variables, where we belong.

Footprints Along the Path

In the morning dew's embrace,
Footprints mark the quiet trail.
Stories whisper in each trace,
Memories of those who prevail.

Sunrise paints the world anew,
Colors dance in warm delight.
Every step we take is true,
Casting shadows in the light.

Leaves rustle with a gentle sigh,
Nature's rhythm, soft and slow.
As the clouds drift in the sky,
Our hopes and dreams begin to grow.

Mountains rise, a steadfast guide,
Beneath their peaks, we find our way.
In the journey, hearts abide,
Walking hand in hand each day.

Through the valleys, deep and wide,
Together we embrace the fight.
Each footprint, stronger with pride,
Leads us to the stars at night.

The Garden of Empathy

In the garden where hearts entwine,
Blooms of kindness softly speak.
Every petal, a gentle sign,
Of love and hope for the meek.

Sunlight streams through leaves so green,
Nurturing all that grows within.
In each corner, peace is seen,
A refuge from the world's din.

Butterflies flit from bud to bud,
Carrying whispers on the breeze.
In this haven, we find our flood,
Of compassion, warmth, and ease.

With every seed of trust we sow,
We blossom kindness, day by day.
Tending each heart's gentle glow,
In our garden, love holds sway.

Together, we watch the flowers rise,
Painting a tapestry of grace.
In the garden, endless skies,
Reflecting every heart's embrace.

Melodies of the Soul

In the stillness of the night,
Whispers of the heart resound.
Melodies take gentle flight,
In the silence, peace is found.

Rhythms dance upon the breeze,
Notes of joy and sorrow blend.
In each heartbeat, we find ease,
Music moments, we can mend.

Strings and keys unite as one,
Harmonies that lift the day.
In this symphony begun,
We share our dreams along the way.

Voices rise to touch the sky,
Echoed in the stars above.
In each stanza, we can fly,
Finding strength through endless love.

Together, we create a song,
Lifting spirits, bright and whole.
In this chorus, we belong,
Singing out the truth—our soul.

Resilience in Unity

In the face of strife and doubt,
We stand strong, hand in hand.
With each challenge, we turn about,
Resilient hearts, a steadfast band.

Through storms that try to tear apart,
We link our strength, unyielding chains.
In unity, we spark the heart,
Transforming struggles into gains.

With every trial that we face,
We rise together, spirits bold.
In this journey, we find our place,
A tapestry of stories told.

From ashes, we shall rise anew,
Like flowers blooming after rain.
In our spirit, hope shines through,
In this resilience, we remain.

Together, we embrace the fight,
Changing shadows into light.
In this dance of life, so bright,
We find our way, we take our flight.

A Symphony of Shared Dreams

In every whisper, hopes take flight,
We weave our wishes, day and night.
Together we paint the skies so bright,
A melody of hearts, pure delight.

Each note a promise, each chord a bond,
Through stormy seas, our spirits respond.
United we stand, of this, we are fond,
In the symphony of dreams, we abscond.

With every heartbeat, our vision grows,
The path ahead, where love overflows.
In harmony, through highs and lows,
Our shared dreams bloom like a timeless rose.

As seasons change, our dreams adapt,
In gentle rhythms, we find the map.
Together we rise, in worlds unwrapped,
In a symphony of love, forever trapped.

So let us cherish this wondrous song,
With hands entwined, we'll carry along.
In a dance of dreams, where we belong,
Our symphony plays, forever strong.

Guiding Stars in Each Other's Sky

When shadows fall and nights grow cold,
Your light shines bright, more precious than gold.
In darkest hours, our stories unfold,
Together we shine, brave and bold.

As twinkling stars, we light the way,
Through tempests fierce, come what may.
In your warmth, my fears decay,
Together we chase the dawn of day.

Though miles may part, our dreams align,
In every heartbeat, your strength is mine.
In this vast universe, beautifully divine,
You are the star, forever I'll shine.

In cosmic dances, we find our tune,
With every heartbeat, morning to noon.
Together we dream beneath the moon,
Guided by stars, our love in bloom.

As galaxies spin, we hold on tight,
In shared constellations, there's endless light.
Forever together, hearts taking flight,
With you by my side, the world feels right.

The Gift of Listening

In quiet moments, I hear your heart,
A gentle whisper, a work of art.
Each story shared, a precious part,
In the gift of listening, love will start.

With open ears, I stand beside,
In your struggles, I won't hide.
In shared silence, feelings collide,
Through the gift of listening, truth is tied.

Your laughter dances, bright and clear,
In your sorrow, I draw near.
With every word, I hold you dear,
The gift of listening, a bond sincere.

In every moment, we choose to pause,
With every heartbeat, we find the cause.
Together we blossom, forever ours,
Through the gift of listening, love empowers.

So speak your truth, my friend, so fine,
In your darkest hours, let your heart shine.
With tender patience, we'll entwine,
In the gift of listening, love divine.

Reflections of Loyalty

In every glance, your truth I see,
A mirror held, reflecting thee.
Through trials faced, you stand with me,
In the dance of loyalty, we're free.

Through storms and sunshine, always near,
With every challenge, we persevere.
In whispered vows, loyalty's clear,
Together we rise, dismissing fear.

In the tapestry of life, threads align,
Every memory, a precious sign.
In laughter shared, our souls entwine,
In reflections of loyalty, we shine.

In every moment, a promise kept,
In silent support, where dreams are adept.
Through shadows cast, our light has leapt,
In the loyal bond, our hearts have crept.

So here we stand, strong and true,
In every heartbeat, my heart knows you.
With open arms, we'll chase the blue,
Reflections of loyalty, forever in view.

The Rhythm of Togetherness

In every heartbeat, we find our song,
Together we dance, where we belong.
With hands entwined, we lead the way,
In the rhythm of life, we choose to stay.

Through trials and joy, we share the load,
Creating memories on this winding road.
With laughter and tears, we grow each day,
In the rhythm of togetherness, come what may.

Every step forward, we face as one,
In the warmth of the sun, our fears undone.
With trust unbroken, we brave the night,
In the rhythm of love, we find our light.

As seasons change, so does our tune,
Yet in the dance, we find our boon.
With hearts wide open, we embrace the flow,
In the rhythm of togetherness, we glow.

No journey too far, no moment too small,
In our togetherness, we conquer all.
With each passing note, our spirits soar,
In the rhythm of life, forevermore.

A Haven of Trust

In whispered secrets, our souls entwine,
A haven of trust, where hearts align.
With gentle hands, we mend each scar,
In this sacred space, we heal from afar.

Through storms we gather, side by side,
In the face of doubt, we will not hide.
With open hearts, we share our fears,
In a haven of trust, we dry our tears.

Each moment savored, every glance held dear,
In this refuge of warmth, there is no fear.
With loyalty planted, we rise as one,
In a haven of trust, our journeys begun.

As shadows linger, we shine our light,
In unity's embrace, we conquer night.
With every word spoken, we nurture the flame,
In a haven of trust, love knows no shame.

Together we whisper, together we dream,
In a haven of trust, we rise and beam.
With each step forward, our bond will grow,
In this sacred space, we always know.

Forests of Compassion

In the depths of the woods, hearts intertwine,
Forests of compassion, both yours and mine.
With every rustle, life softly speaks,
In nature's embrace, the spirit peaks.

Beneath towering trees, we share our woes,
In every leaf's whisper, our understanding grows.
With gratitude blooming, we find our peace,
In these forests of compassion, we find release.

With branches reaching, we shelter each tear,
In the shade of growth, we conquer our fear.
With every soft step, our journey unfolds,
In these forests of compassion, our story's told.

As the seasons change, we stand side by side,
In nature's rhythm, we take our stride.
With roots like anchors, we flourish and thrive,
In the forests of compassion, we come alive.

Through challenges faced, we nurture the soil,
In the heart of the woods, our spirits uncoil.
With love as our guide, we endlessly roam,
In these forests of compassion, we've found our home.

Conversations Under Canopies

Beneath the branches, we share our dreams,
Conversations bloom like gentle streams.
With laughter dancing on the air so sweet,
In the world's embrace, our hearts compete.

As sunlight filters through the leaves so bright,
We weave our stories in pure delight.
With every word spoken, our spirits soar,
In conversations under canopies, we explore.

The rustle of leaves becomes our song,
In moments like these, we know we belong.
With trust as our anchor, we delve so deep,
In conversations under canopies, secrets keep.

With shadows playing as the day does fade,
We share our hopes, in soft glades we wade.
With dreams like whispers, we reach for the sky,
In conversations under canopies, we fly.

As stars twinkle above, the night grows near,
In the warmth of friendship, we conquer fear.
With hearts intertwined, the universe vast,
In conversations under canopies, love will last.

Unseen Threads of Connection

In silence we share the same breath,
Invisible lines that bind us tight.
With every glance, a shared truth,
In the shadows, our hearts ignite.

Through laughter and tears, we weave,
A tapestry rich with our dreams.
Though miles apart, we believe,
In the bond that silently gleams.

Whispers on the wind unite,
Time and space cannot sever.
Our spirits dance in the light,
Together, now and forever.

In the depths of the night sky,
Stars echo stories we hold dear.
Through the darkness, we will fly,
The unseen threads always near.

Connected by fate's gentle hand,
In a world vast and unknown.
We are stronger, we understand,
Together, we are never alone.

The Language of Togetherness

In every smile, a story unfolds,
In every touch, a bond is formed.
The laughter echoes, warm and bold,
In the heart, our love keeps us warmed.

Words unspoken, yet we know,
A glance reveals what we can't say.
In quiet moments, feelings flow,
Together, we find our way.

When hurdles rise, we hold on tight,
With every challenge, we grow strong.
In unity, we find our light,
Together, we've known where we belong.

The rhythm of our hearts, in sync,
In harmony, our spirits soar.
In the depths of life, we think,
That together, we can explore.

Through thick and thin, we share our dreams,
In every struggle, side by side.
The language of love softly beams,
Together, there's nothing to hide.

Companionship's Compass

In the journey of life, we walk hand in hand,
Navigating paths both wild and grand.
With each step taken, our hearts align,
In the compass of love, your heart is mine.

Through storms and sunshine, we steer our ship,
With hopes that anchor and dreams that equip.
In laughter's embrace, we find our way,
Companionship's glow lights our day.

Moments of silence, we cherish so dear,
In the stillness, our souls draw near.
With every memory, we build our map,
In the treasure of friendship, we share a lap.

As seasons change, we grow together,
Finding solace in any weather.
In the dance of life, we twirl and sway,
Our compass forever guides our way.

Through mountains high and valleys low,
In each adventure, our spirits grow.
In the heart of companionship, we find bliss,
A journey enriched by every kiss.

Cherished Moments

In the gentle hush of evening's glow,
We pause to breathe, to take it slow.
Every glance shared, a fleeting spark,
In the quiet, we leave our mark.

With laughter warm and stories spun,
We gather moments, one by one.
In simple joys, our hearts take flight,
Cherished memories, pure and bright.

Through sunlit days and starlit nights,
We chase the magic, the heart's delights.
In every heartbeat, a promise made,
In cherished moments, love will never fade.

When time stands still, we savor the best,
In shared glances, we find our rest.
With every whisper, our souls entwine,
In treasured moments, forever shine.

As time rolls on, we'll hold them tight,
These cherished moments, our guiding light.
In the tapestry of life we weave,
In love's embrace, we always believe.

Milton Keynes UK
Ingram Content Group UK Ltd.
UKHW021208261024
450281UK00007B/109

9 789916 891063